RAIL

BRITISH COLUMBIA'S
GREAT TRAIN ADVENTURE

CHRIS HARRIS

COUNTRY LIGHT PUBLISHING

Copyright 1993 by Chris Harris

All rights reserved. No part of this book may be reproduced in any way without prior written permission of the publisher.

All photography by Chris Harris except for page 91 by BC Rail
"Pacific Great Eastern to BC Rail" by Elaine Jones
"All Aboard—Vancouver to Prince George!" by Elaine Jones & Syd Cannings

Edited by Darlene Calyniuk
Designed by Vic Marks
Typeset by The Typeworks, Vancouver, B.C.
Printed and bound in Hong Kong

Canadian Cataloguing in Publication Data

Harris, Chris, 1939
   BC Rail
ISBN 0-9695235-1-3

   1. BC Rail—History—Pictorial works. 2. Railroads—British Columbia—History—Pictorial works. 3. BC Rail—Pictorial works. 4. Railroads—British Columbia—Pictorial works. 5. Natural history—British Columbia—Pictorial works. I. Title.
HE2810.B75H37 1993   385ƒ.06ƒ5711   c93-091445-7

To order autographed copies of this book and others in the series "Discovering British Columbia," contact:

Country Light Publishing
c-333, 108 Mile Ranch, B.C. V0K 2Z0

Phone: (604) 791-6631, or Fax: (604) 791-6671

No. 4601 passes by a sheep bluff near Mile 174, where, moments before, a large California bighorn ram stood overlooking the beautiful sagebrush country north of Lillooet.

To the memory of my mother,
who travelled everywhere by train,
and whose wonderful free spirit encouraged me
to travel and explore.

Near Mile 183 the Fraser River, nearly two thousand feet below, appears to be a mere stream. The BC Rail mainline has been described by many international rail travellers as the most scenic of any railroad in the world.

CONTENTS

ACKNOWLEDGEMENTS
11

From Pacific Great Eastern to BC Rail—1912 to the 1990s
12

Map
13

The Royal Hudson Steam Train
43

All Aboard—Vancouver to Prince George!
59

SOURCES FOR INFORMATION
96

From Vancouver to Prince George, the line passes through sixteen tunnels. This is the train engineer's view, as the setting sun lights up the tunnel's interior.

Acknowledgements

One of my greatest pleasures in photographing this book was meeting so many friendly employees of BC Rail. Many shared fascinating stories collected during their long careers with the company. Others contributed ideas and assistance in many forms. Without their help, many of the photographs in this book would not have been possible. Special thanks go to John Alexander, Fred Belding, Olin Ford, Bill Lukoni, Doug Martin, Ken Mason, Don McGregor, Bill Merry, Jake Morrison, Ralph Odendahl, Rob Pearson, Steve Pudney, Walter Raspberry, Ross Regan, Lee Sheppard, Joe Smuin, Randy Westgate, Pat Wheeldon, and the many others whose names I have missed.

I am also grateful to Noel van Sandwyk and Barrie Wall at BC Rail's head office, who opened many doors.

A number of close friends also helped with ideas, enthusiasm and support of many kinds: Ken and Betty Cairns, Mike and Darlene Calyniuk, Tom Ellison, Pat Hancock, Jenny Harris, Bob Herger, Dean Hull, and Gerry and Marie Weldon. Thanks also to the knowledgeable staff at Lens and Shutter and Custom Color.

I would like to specially acknowledge the work of Syd Cannings and Elaine Jones, who have written the text for the book. Their contributions add much to the understanding of this remarkable railway journey.

Many thanks go to publishers Vic Marks and Gordon Soules, who continue to share their considerable experience and knowledge of publishing.

At 7:30 a.m. passengers aboard the Cariboo Express leave the North Vancouver station on the 460-mile journey to Prince George. The Royal Hudson awaits its departure a little later in the day.

From Pacific Great Eastern to BC Rail—1912 to the 1990s

A hundred years ago, if you wanted to travel overland from Vancouver to Prince George—or Fort George as it was known until 1915—you would prepare for a rough, uncomfortable, and difficult journey by river steamer and stagecoach. Today this trip takes just over thirteen hours, in the air-conditioned comfort of self-propelled rail coaches called Budd cars. This one-day journey passes through some of British Columbia's most breathtaking scenery, much of it almost untouched, and is made all the more amazing because of the rapid transitions between geographic zones. Even the neophyte naturalist can detect the differences in topography and vegetation along the way, and the variety of communities tells another story, about the settlement patterns and industrial development of the province.

The history and development of British Columbia over the last century has been intimately connected with railways, and remains so today. In 1912, when Conservative Premier Richard McBride proposed a new provincial railway linking Vancouver with Fort George, he envisioned a line that would eventually extend right to the border with Alaska. McBride's Pacific Great Eastern Railway, named after Britain's Great Eastern Railway, would do for British Columbia's north and interior what the CPR had done for Canada's west. Most particularly, it would open up the rich natural resources of the hinterland and link the burgeoning agricultural Peace River district to the coast. As it happened, the laying of track to Prince George took four decades to complete, earning his Pacific Great Eastern Railway (PGE) one of its many tongue-in-cheek names, "Prince George Eventually."

From the beginning, the railway faced difficulties. Conceived in the flush of prosperity, it was soon plagued with economic problems. The beginning of World War One came at a critical time for the struggling railway and the worldwide economic depression of the following years further delayed development. While surveyors worked their way through the wilderness to determine just how difficult the laying of track would be through this rugged country, Premier McBride was facing another kind of hurdle at the beginning of the line. In 1912, irate residents of the newly incorporated District of West Vancouver petitioned to have the route diverted from the foreshore; after a stalemate of several months and appointment of a commission to settle the question, McBride took a firm stand and the route was unchanged.

The first spike was driven on the North Shore line in October 1913. The following summer there was service between North Vancouver and Whytecliff in present-day West Vancouver—about twelve miles of track. Meanwhile, surveying continued at both ends of the railway. By 1916, a line was operating between Squamish and Clinton. But over the next few years, development of the railway proceeded in fits and starts: the growing depression of the twenties and thirties meant that progress on the last miles of the line—stalled for decades by the difficult crossing of the Cottonwood River—and repairs to existing track were put on hold. By 1928, the line between North Vancouver and Whytecliff was no longer in operation.

In 1929, a twice-weekly run between Squamish and Quesnel was barely keeping the railway afloat. Ironically, Cariboo farmers began shipping produce in greater amounts than ever before. In the depths of the Depression, McBride's dream of opening up the resources of the Interior was being realized in at least one small way.

West of Lillooet lies the little town of Bralorne. Now virtually a ghost town, discovery of gold here in 1933 meant renewed life for the flagging railway. Equipment and vehicles

B.C. Rail provides commercial and tourist services throughout its system.

The Royal Hudson steam train travels only the first 39 miles between Vancouver and Squamish. The Cariboo Express Dayliner offers a 462 mile adventure from Vancouver to Prince George. Freight trains and occasional passenger specialty tours travel throughtout the rail system.

for the mine were transported from Lillooet to Shalalth, where they were unloaded to make the tortuous trek by road to the mines. From 1925 to 1946 the railway was offered on the world market with incentives such as large land grants along the right of way, but there were no takers and the railway remained in the province's reluctant hands. The PGE gained a new name: "Province's Greatest Expense."

The beginning of the Second World War brought increased business, as timber was shipped south for the war effort. The postwar economic boom of the late forties, with its emphasis on exploitation of mineral and forest resources, saw the first spurt of growth for the railway in many years. Pushing the line on to Peace River country, a promise made since 1912, began to seem like a reality when the provincial government committed to a northern development plan. Preliminary surveying began in 1946 on the section between Prince George and the Azouzetta River.

An acceptable crossing for the notorious Cottonwood River was finally found, and the first train made the run from Quesnel to Prince George on September 11, 1952. A large crowd assembled to greet the inaugural train as it entered Prince George with great fanfare on November 1 that year. Surveyor L.C. Gunn, who had mapped the preliminary route in 1912, drove the last spike. By January, freight service was established and passenger service began that spring between Squamish and Prince George.

The railway began to make the switch from steam to diesel in 1947, marking the end of a railway era. Today a remnant of that time can be experienced on the Royal Hudson, which runs between North Vancouver and Squamish during the summer months.

With the line to Prince George finally completed, the next task was to close the forty-mile gap between North Vancouver and Squamish. It was no wonder this section had been left for last. The sheer cliffs and unforgiving topography of Howe Sound were a nightmare for surveyors. In addition, the residents of West Vancouver rose once again in protest against the reopening of the line through the municipality. During the intervening decades, the disused right of way had been adapted to urban use, with gardens, garages and play areas. Once again, the PGE had to smooth ruffled feathers, but by 1956, the original charter of the PGE was fulfilled: rails ran uninterrupted from North Vancouver to Prince George.

By 1972, when its name was changed to BC Rail, the railway was proving its mettle. Freight could be shipped from Fort Nelson to Vancouver by 1971, and in 1990 the total length of track was 1,387 miles. While the passenger service is well-known to the general public—particularly the nostalgic Royal Hudson run—and serves an important function for B.C. residents and tourists, the dream of realizing the potential of northern British Columbia is proved by the figures. In the early 1990s, the passenger service accounted for only 1 percent of the railway's revenues; freight accounted for the rest, with shipment of forestry products at 62 percent, and coal, at 20 percent, forming the bulk.

PREVIOUS LEAF: *A freight train snakes downhill to Lillooet, at about Mile 168.*

OPPOSITE: *Mountain goats and bighorn sheep get this perspective of the Budd cars as they wind their way north, skirting the shoreline of Anderson and Seton lakes. The relatively small dayliner cars are walled in by steep cliffs on one side and glacial waters on the other.*

OVERLEAF: *Grain elevators and freight lines at Dawson Creek, Mile 0 of the Alaska Highway. Some of B.C.'s finest farmland is situated in this northeastern part of the province.*

PREVIOUS LEAF: *A freight train crosses the Peace River bridge amid a blaze of fall colour. By 1958 BC Rail had pioneered a route from Prince George north through Pine Pass to Chetwynd, Dawson Creek and Fort St. John. Until then, the rich resources of northern B.C. had lain dormant, awaiting access to world markets.*

Mirrored in the calm water of the Peace River, an early-morning freight moves slowly through the mist. The only river in Canada to breach the Rockies, the Peace was once the route for furs moving eastward.

PREVIOUS LEAF: *The forty miles north of Lillooet, along the Fraser Canyon, provides some of B.C.'s most dramatic and awe-inspiring scenery.*

OPPOSITE: *Looking tiny in comparison to the expansive Cariboo Plateau country and the huge trestles of the Deep Creek Bridge, three Budd cars cross the bridge at Mile 330. It is one of the highest railway bridges in the world at 312 feet.*

OVERLEAF: *The unusually still waters of Anderson Lake form a near-perfect reflection of the surrounding mountains.*

OPPOSITE, ABOVE: *The route along Anderson and Seton lakes is both spectacular and dangerous—it is notorious for slides, and derailments of freight trains have occurred. The rugged mountains provide excellent habitat for mountain goats and sheep, which can be spotted by sharp-eyed passengers.*

The stretch from Fountain to Kelly Lake is the longest climb of 2.2 percent grade in North America—a steady ascent for thirty-five miles. It's an exciting journey for cross-country skiers bound for the central Cariboo area, which sports the most extensive cross-country ski trail system in western Canada.

OPPOSITE, ABOVE: *Clinging to the narrowest of ledges, the train corners a sixteen-degree curve—the sharpest turn on the entire mainline. A yellow speeder precedes every train along this dangerous section of track, scouting for boulders or major rock slides on the tracks.*

OVERLEAF: *In the hours just before daybreak, with the temperature dipping well below zero, No. 4620 pushes north between Clinton and 100 Mile House.*

OPPOSITE, ABOVE: *Budd cars cross Cheakamus Canyon, in the heart of the Coast Mountains. Travellers can't help but develop a respect for the early surveyors who found the routes of least resistance through this difficult terrain and the construction crews who later laid the track.*

OVERLEAF: *A dusting of snow emphasizes the patterns of erosion. During the past 10,000 years, the Fraser River has continued to carve out its chasm, nearly 3,000 feet deep in places, along the Fraser River Fault line.*

The Royal Hudson Steam Train

The romance of the great era of train travel lives on in the Royal Hudson steam train, No. 2860, which operates a passenger service between North Vancouver and Squamish during the summer months.

The Royal Hudson is one of the Hudson-type locomotives built between 1929 and 1940 for high-speed passenger service across Canada in the late steam era. In 1939, during the celebrated cross-Canada tour of King George VI and Queen Elizabeth, its sister engine, No. 2850, was chosen to head the Royal train. The engine performed admirably, without a single malfunction between Quebec and Vancouver, so impressing the CPR that permission was asked and granted to add the "Royal" designation to the streamlined models of the Hudson locomotives. Crowns were affixed to all the engines, thereafter known as Royal Hudsons.

The Hudsons were among the most handsome engines ever built, and their construction provided high traction and better high-speed efficiency. The 2860 spent sixteen years powering trains through the difficult terrain between Vancouver and Revelstoke. But the era of steam was over, and the 2860, like all the other Hudsons, was consigned to the scrap heap. A reprieve came in 1964, when it was restored as part of a proposed railway museum in Vancouver, but when the museum project fell through, the engine sat for another decade in storage.

The provincial government eventually bought the 2860, with the aim of returning the locomotive to active service. Another year went by while it was being restored, and in 1974, the Royal Hudson took its inaugural run. Since that time the train has made three major tours: to Washington State, Oregon and California in 1977, eastern Canada in 1978, and the Pacific Northwest in 1979. Everywhere it went, the Royal Hudson excited great interest.

The 2860, the only steam locomotive still in scheduled mainline service in North America, has proved to be one of British Columbia's greatest attractions. Some 100,000 passengers a year board the Royal Hudson in North Vancouver for the eighty-mile round trip to Squamish and back—not only to experience the romance of travel under steam, but to enjoy one of the most scenic routes in British Columbia.

The Royal Hudson sports the provincial coat of arms.

OPPOSITE: *The Royal Hudson, No. 2860, steams across the Furry Creek bridge at Mile 28. This locomotive is the lone operating survivor of sixty-five Hudson-type engines that operated a high-speed passenger service across Canada at the end of the steam era.*

The Royal Hudson, seen from the waters of Howe Sound. As well as an opportunity to see the spectacular scenery on the day trip to Squamish, the Royal Hudson provides fully restored steam-era passenger cars, including the open-windowed observation car.

OPPOSITE: *The engineer keeps a close eye on the Royal Hudson's many gauges, which indicate such things as steam, boiler, and cylinder pressures. The Royal Hudson, weighing 366,000 pounds, has a water capacity of 12,000 gallons—good for 150 miles.*

The Royal Hudson sways along tracks carved into solid cliffs above the shores of the Pacific Ocean. It's customary to sound the whistle here, which brings residents of Lions Bay out onto their balconies to wave a friendly greeting to visitors from around the world.

OPPOSITE: *The power of steam is manifest as the Royal Hudson bursts forth from one of six tunnels on its way to Squamish.*

OVERLEAF: *During the early-morning hours, several engineers go through the ritual preparation of the Royal Hudson for its daily, eighty-mile return journey.*

ABOVE, OPPOSITE: *The power and drama of the steam engine is emphasized as it emerges from a tunnel, surrounded by billowing plumes of smoke.*

ABOVE, OPPOSITE: *A nostalgic reminder of the way travel used to be. The stationmaster's desk, from a 1914 Grand Trunk Railway Station, is part of the Prince George Railway Museum. The photo on the right recalls a typical sight for a stationmaster of that time.*

OVERLEAF: *Stawamus Chief looms in the background near Mile 39. The Chief is an international climbing destination and climbers can sometimes be seen clinging to its sheer face.*

The world-famous Royal Hudson looks small in comparison to the majestic surroundings of Howe Sound. The Royal Hudson is currently the sole steam locomotive in scheduled mainline passenger service in North America; over 100,000 people ride this route each year.

An engineer makes a final check of the oil level. The fuel capacity is 4,100 gallons, with a mileage range of 450 miles.

All Aboard—Vancouver to Prince George!

The BC Rail passenger service from Vancouver to Prince George is an ideal way to see a one-day cross-section of British Columbia—from tidewater to the geographic centre of the province. While the train eats up the miles, passengers can relax and watch thousands of years of history roll past the windows. The line passes through magnificent mountain ranges, travels alongside spectacular canyons, and traverses the interior plateau. Naturally, with this diverse habitat, there are opportunities to see a variety of wildlife species, and animal-spotting is a frequent pastime along the route.

Through the Coast Mountains—Vancouver to Lillooet

Thanks to Premier McBride's decision to keep the original right of way, today's BCR passengers have a privileged start to their journey. The train pulls out of the North Vancouver depot promptly at 7 a.m. The dawn is still fresh, touching the downtown towers with a rosy hue as the train passes under the Lions Gate Bridge. The line follows closely along the shoreline, affording panoramic views of the harbour dotted with waiting freighters and closeups of joggers along the seawall. Picking up speed, the train moves inland through the residential area. Houses appear surprisingly close: lighted windows flash by like frames in a movie, allowing brief voyeuristic glimpses of people drinking their morning coffee and making toast.

After the Horseshoe Bay Tunnel—the longest tunnel on the mainline to Prince George, at 4,500 feet—the train emerges above Horseshoe Bay and heads up Howe Sound. Snow-capped mountain vistas open up ahead; ferries, pleasure craft and tugs ply the waters below.

The train sways along on tracks apparently carved into solid cliffs. The steep walls of Howe Sound, a classic glacial fiord, were carved by massive rivers of ice flowing out of the mountains. Fifteen thousand years ago, ice up to 8,000 feet thick covered this entire area, and evidence of its tremendous erosive power can be seen everywhere. The tops of the lower summits have been smoothed and domed by the actions of the glaciers. In summer, the perpetually ice-clad summits of the Tantalus Range to the west are a reminder that there are still remnants of Ice Age glaciers in these mountains.

It's impossible to ride this route without developing a healthy respect for the pioneer surveyors who were responsible for laying these tracks. Using the most primitive of instruments, their innate knowledge of terrain and an understanding of track-laying costs, they were expected to find the safest and most economical routes through an almost impenetrable wilderness. Much of today's track is laid according to the original survey plans completed near the beginning of the century.

The present Coast Mountains are very young geologically and are actually the second mountain range to rise along this shore. The original range eroded away long ago, but left beneath it a core consisting of a huge batholith—a body of magma that cooled and crystallized far beneath the surface.

OPPOSITE: *Passengers bound for the resort town of Whistler revel in the sight of fresh snow along the route.*

OVERLEAF: *Homeward bound, the Cariboo Express approaches Porteau Cove Park. Campers in the park can often be seen enjoying a meal while overlooking the fabulous scenery of Howe Sound.*

This core was exposed during the recent rapid uplift that occurred over the past few million years, and most of the present range is composed of this granitic rock. A magnificent example is the Stawamus Chief just east of the railway at Squamish; another example is the canyon of the Cheakamus River north of Squamish.

This part of the Coast Mountains makes up the northern curve of the Cascade volcanic arc, and evidence of recent volcanic activity surrounds the traveller. Mount Garibaldi is the shattered remnant of a large volcano formed near the close of the Ice Ages, some 12,000 years ago. The train passenger can see extensive lava flows in the form of angular basalt columns and rubble along the tracks as the train nears Whistler, and Brandywine Creek plunges 280 feet over a vertical basalt wall only a few feet from the railway bridge at the brink of the falls.

The forests here are dominated by huge Douglas-firs, identifiable by their thick, furrowed bark and broken tops—perfect perches for the many bald eagles that frequent the coast. The other common coniferous species are western hemlock and western redcedar. Big-leaf maples and red alders are common broadleaf trees.

The Squamish River estuary is home to many waterfowl species, including a population of wintering trumpeter swans. Salmon move up the river and its tributaries in late autumn and early winter; by mid-January the streams are filled with their spent bodies. This sets the stage for one of North America's great midwinter wildlife spectacles, when over 1,000 bald eagles gather to feast on salmon carcasses.

Past Squamish the train begins the climb through the Coast Mountains—2,100 feet in thirty-four miles. The track curves along the Cheakamus River, its ascent affording stunning views of Cheakamus Canyon as the train twists along narrow ledges on the steep-sided cliff. Waterfalls, pools, turbulent rapids, sculpted cliffs where trees precariously cling—the landscape possesses a compelling beauty. In places the cliffs seem to pass within inches of the train's windows.

Near the summit of the grade is the Whistler station, a major resort destination for passengers. Whistler marks the divide of the outer range of the Coast Mountains. In winter, the combination of colder air from the Interior and moist air coming off the Pacific Ocean results in impressive snowfalls, especially at higher elevations. This is the heart of one of the snowiest areas on earth. Even though the interior mountains of British Columbia have much colder winters and shorter summers than the Coast Mountains, timberline here on the coast is considerably lower than in the Interior. For small plants, the growing season at Whistler is determined not by the frost-free period, but by the snow-free period. In many years, snow lies over much of the high mountain meadows until mid-July.

Past nearby Alta Lake, the train begins the descent into the Pemberton Valley, cradled between two ranges of the Coast

PREVIOUS LEAF: *Looking out over Howe Sound from Porteau Cove Park.*

OPPOSITE: *A seven-car dayliner slowly winds its way up Cheakamus Canyon along a narrow band of steel precariously built halfway up the cliffside.*

OVERLEAF: *Passengers are familiar with conductors, baggage handlers and even engineers, but they rarely see the dedicated crew that works behind the scenes to ensure the safety of the route. They check, repair and maintain the lines, and some operate the speeder that precedes trains from Mile 0 to Mile 191 near Kelly Lake. They have prevented many major accidents over the years.*

PREVIOUS LEAF: *Near Mile 255, the line passes one of the oldest barns in the Cariboo. Located close to 150 Mile on the gold rush trail, it is slowly collapsing after over one hundred years of heavy winter snows.*

From northern B.C., a freight train starts its long journey southward through an eery morning fog.

Mountains. Surrounded by the serrated edges of mountain peaks, the lush valley supports ranching, farming and forestry. From Pemberton, the train ascends again to Birken, running alongside the beautiful Birkenhead River for much of the distance. The unusually clear water flows over a riverbed of multicoloured rocks, where spawning salmon are visible.

The track follows the shore of Anderson and Seton lakes closely for their entire thirty-two-mile length. This area is notorious for slides, and a yellow "speeder" can be seen running along ahead of the train, scouting for problems on the track. Across the lakes, there is often evidence of recent slides—fresh earth in narrow defiles and piles of debris at shore level. In 1950, a train derailed and plunged into Anderson Lake, killing the engineer and conductor. The last serious derailment occurred in 1980, when a slide caused a freight locomotive to derail and sink into Seton Lake. The two lakes, once one long lake, are separated by a narrow neck of land created by a huge landslide.

Passengers are sometimes puzzled by the dramatic colour difference between the lakes. Anderson has clear, deep blue water, while Seton is the milky greenish hue typical of glacier-fed lakes. This may seem unusual at first, since Seton Lake is downstream of Anderson, but the puzzle is answered at South Shalalth, where tunnels and penstocks bring glacial water

Only a few feet separates the cold waters of Seton Lake from the steep rock wall behind a northbound dayliner.

OVERLEAF: *Long freight trains, often pulling more than a hundred cars, carry goods from central and northern B.C. Forest products represent over 60 percent of total freight revenue, while mining, manufacturing, agriculture and intermodal services make up the balance. This southbound freight is making the steepest thirty-mile descent in North America.*

through the mountains from Carpenter Lake to feed the power station on Seton's shores.

The rugged mountains surrounding Anderson and Seton lakes expose rock faces that symbolize the geological history of much of British Columbia. They are foreign rocks that collided with North America about 150 million years ago. These mountains, like all those of western British Columbia, were thrust upward when another chunk of the earth's crust (including Vancouver Island) collided with the west coast of North America about 50 million years later. Today, mountain goats enjoy the security offered by the craggy cliffs; watch for their shaggy white coats on the bluffs along Seton Lake.

Along the Fraser Canyon—Lillooet to Clinton

As the track descends the dry side of the Coast Mountains toward Lillooet, the change in terrain and vegetation becomes obvious. The lush coastal forests and jagged snow-capped peaks of the coast give way to sparsely treed slopes and dry sagebrush country.

Once a booming gold rush town—Mile 0 on the trail to the Cariboo gold fields—Lillooet is now a centre for surrounding cattlelands and ginseng farms. Just past Lillooet, concrete fish ladders bypass rapids and the drying racks of native fishers on ledges above the water indicate that the Fraser is rich with salmon, although its silt-laden waters obscure any life within. Through the summer and fall, tens of thousands of salmon travel upstream, returning to a number of home streams to spawn before dying. Some of these salmon are chinook that are travelling over 600 miles to their birthplace near the base of Mount Robson in the Rocky Mountains.

The thirty miles past Lillooet encompasses some of B.C.'s most dramatic and awe-inspiring country. In places the track clings to cliffs hundreds of feet above a sheer drop to the river below. The canyon developed along the Fraser River fault, an ancient seam between pieces of the earth's crust, which at Lillooet marks the eastern edge of the Coast Mountains. The fertile benchlands on either side of the river were deposited at the end of the Ice Ages in the bottoms of lakes filled with silty meltwater. In the intervening 10,000 years, the river has continued to carve out its chasm, which in places is 3,000 feet deep.

As the track climbs, it moves back from the canyon's edge, allowing panoramic views of the river as it winds through the deep-walled chasm. The contours of the land are breathtaking, denuded of all extraneous features. Hayfields and the more recent ginseng farms spreading across benchlands high above the Fraser do little to reduce the sense of solitude and grandeur. The track climbs relentlessly for forty-three miles, gaining 2,700 feet, the longest climb at a 2.2 percent grade in North America. At the highest point, just before leaving the Fraser, it is a vertiginous 2,000 feet above the canyon. Nowhere is the skill required of railway builders more obvious.

The deep valley of the Fraser and the rainshadow produced by the Coast Mountains produce the dramatic semi-arid landscape especially noticeable north of Fountain. Expanses of sagebrush are home to songbirds like western meadowlarks and vesper sparrows, and the big ponderosa pines at the edge of the

OPPOSITE: *A northbound freight crosses the Fraser River at Mile 160, just past Lillooet. The river looks calm here, but during spring runoff it rises several feet.*

OVERLEAF: *A "pusher" locomotive, added to assist two engines at the front of the train, crosses Fiftyone Creek Bridge at Mile 206, just north of Clinton.*

OPPOSITE, ABOVE: *Several mountain goats can be seen on the cliffs above No. 4620 as it approaches Lillooet. These agile mountain climbers are often seen here on the western side of the track. As winter approaches, their thick winter coats are in immaculate condition.*

woodlands shelter Lewis's woodpeckers. Watch for these pink-bellied birds perched on the broken, dead tops of trees, waiting for butterflies or other large insects to fly by. Between Pavilion and Moran, steep, grassy slopes are perfect habitat for California bighorn sheep, which can often be spotted from the train—sometimes grazing in hayfields with cattle. The rams have massive, curled horns; the ewes and young have shorter, slimmer horns that are only slightly curved.

The Great Plateau—Clinton to Williams Lake

Leaving the Fraser behind, the route turns east toward Clinton and the vast Cariboo plateau. This is prime ranching country; surrounded by the flattened summits of low-rising mountains, there is a sense of being on top of the world. The Exeter station is near Mile 100, a popular stagecoach stopover during the Cariboo gold rush. Today it is the centre of a ranching and resort area and a popular summer and winter destination for railway passengers.

As the train moves into cooler elevations, the ponderosa pines disappear, and white spruce, the trees of the great northern forests of North America, take their place among the Douglas-fir, trembling aspen and lodgepole pine. In the summer, this forest is carpeted a brilliant green with pine grass and jewelled with the scarlet bracts of Indian paintbrush.

Groups of mule deer—up to twenty at a time—can sometimes be seen bounding away through the woodlands. These interior deer are larger than their coastal cousins, which may be seen along the railway in the Squamish Valley.

About 13 to 25 million years ago, this area was very active volcanically and flow after flow of lava poured over the landscape, eventually forming the flat basalt surface of the Cariboo Plateau that we know today. The huge canyon at Chasm (unfortunately, the train traveller can see only the rim) is an excellent showpiece of these lava layers.

The surface details of the plateau were created during the retreat of glaciers, which left a mantle of rocks and gravel behind. Blocks of ice caused depressions in this surface. When the ice melted, lakes or wetlands formed. Surrounded by lush shorelines of sedges, rushes, cattails and willows, these wetlands are home to thousands of waterfowl. Heading toward Williams Lake, the railway follows the marshy and meandering San Jose River through open aspen parkland and wetlands. In the summer, this country is alive with many kinds of birds, including American kestrels, black terns, mountain bluebirds, western meadowlarks, and several kinds of flycatchers and swallows.

Beaver dams and lodges are also plentiful. Watch for the distinctively gnawed ends of trees to see where beaver are at work. Other wildlife that may be visible include foxes and coyotes, which can be seen loping across the fields, and lucky travellers may see moose, the largest deer, wading in the shallows.

Northern Forests—Williams Lake to Prince George

At Williams Lake, the line rejoins the Fraser, heading north on the last stage of its journey. Travelling north, signs of the forest industry increase markedly: pulp mills, chipping operations,

PREVIOUS LEAF: *Trains make a careful approach to a series of the sharpest turns along the entire BC Rail route, near Mile 150.*

OPPOSITE: *Throughout the Cariboo region, from Clinton to Prince George, the train passes through forested areas inundated with hundreds of lakes and sloughs. A keen observer can spot beaver lodges and dams, deer, coyotes, foxes, black bears—or moose, as they run from the passing train.*

ABOVE, OPPOSITE: *Passengers with an interest in natural history will be fascinated by the ever-changing land forms.*

OVERLEAF: *The Fraser River north of Williams Lake. The track follows the Fraser River to Quesnel, the route used by paddlewheelers taking goods and prospectors to the gold fields.*

beehive burners and logging trucks. The train passes through industrial areas of urban centres where the smell of wood hangs in the air and smokestacks spew particles skyward. McBride's dream of opening up the interior has been realized in centres such as Williams Lake, Quesnel and Prince George, where forestry is a mainstay of the economy.

Birds are plentiful in this region, and ospreys are often seen along the tracks here. Their nests are easy to identify, consisting of a big stack of sticks at the very top of a tree or other support. Canada geese show a preference for raising their families in vacant osprey nests, and since they usually begin to nest before ospreys, the unlucky osprey landlords are forced to build new accommodations. At a plywood factory south of Quesnel, watch for two nests on the top of light standards near the tracks.

North of Quesnel, the railroad enters the boreal forests once more. The moist climate is well illustrated by extensive bogs near the small centre of Cinema. Look for open expanses of mossy muskeg sparsely treed with slender, stunted black spruce.

Older white spruces can be recognized from a distance by the heavy, droopy appearance of the branches. Lodgepole pine is common in areas earlier burned by forest fires. Paper birch indicates moist areas with poor drainage. The other common tree of this forest is the trembling aspen, a beautiful, white-barked deciduous tree with quivering leaves the size and shape of dollar coins. In the autumn, aspens turn a glorious gold, creating stunning landscapes in combination with the dark evergreens.

A few miles outside Quesnel is the Cottonwood River. In seconds the train has rocketed over the bridge—1,023 feet long and 312 feet above the water—and continues on to Prince George, the terminus of the BCR's passenger service.

OPPOSITE: *Developing British Columbia's northeastern coalfields was the single largest industrial undertaking in the history of the province. BC Rail electrified coal-carrying railway is clean, quiet and non-polluting, and one of only three fifty-kilovolt railway systems in the world. These GF6-Cs p*̲ *one hundred cars, each with a hundred tons of coal.*

The last remaining water tower along the entire route, near Mile 246, is a nostalgic reminder of past rail travel. In the days of steam, towers were located every thirty-five to forty miles along the track. This one was left standing to store water for the small community of Lone Butte.

PREVIOUS LEAF: *A freight train crosses the huge plateau north of the Peace River between Fort St. John and Fort Nelson. This huge, open country is some of B.C.'s best farmland—90 percent of seeded field crops in B.C. are grown here in the Peace country.*

The Cariboo Express speeds past a railway crossing at sunset.

Sources for Information

For information on BC Rail passenger services, write to:

BC Rail
Passenger Services
Box 8770
Vancouver, B.C.   v6b 4x4
CANADA

For information on other books in this series, write to:

Country Light Publishing
c-333
108 Mile Ranch, B.C.
v0k 2z0
CANADA